MARS

SEYMOUR SIMON

MULBERRY BOOKS • New York

PICTURE CREDITS:
All photographs courtesy of
the Jet Propulsion Laboratory
(California Institute of Technology)/NASA,
except page 4, courtesy of
Richard Dreiser, The Yerkes Observatory.
Drawing on page 6 by Todd Radom.

First Mulberry Edition, 1990

Printed in Italy

1 2 3 4 5 6 7 8 9 10

Library of Congress Cataloging-in-Publication Data
Simon, Seymour.
Mars.
Summary: Text and photographs, describe features of
the red planet.
1. Mars (Planet)—Juvenile literature.
[1. Mars (Planet)] I. Title.
QB641.S494   1987   523.4'3   86-31106
ISBN 0-688-09928-9 ·

To H. G. Wells and Edgar Rice Burroughs,
who shaped my childhood visions of Mars

Mars looks like a bright star in the night sky. But Mars is a planet. Mars appears so bright because it is closer to us than any other planet except Venus.

Mars is sometimes called the "Red Planet" because it shines with a reddish or orange color. Two thousand years ago, the planet's red color made the Romans think of blood and war. So the Romans named it Mars, after their god of war.

Mars is the fourth planet from the sun, after Mercury, Venus, and our own planet, Earth. Mars is more than 140 million miles from the sun—50 million miles farther away from the sun than Earth. It is also a smaller planet than Earth, 4,218 miles across. If Earth were hollow, seven planets the size of Mars could fit inside.

Earth and Mars travel around the sun in paths called orbits. Earth takes one year, 365 days, to orbit the sun. But Mars is farther away and takes longer to orbit the sun. A Martian year is 687 Earth days, almost twice as long as a year on Earth. A Martian day is only about half an hour longer than a day on Earth.

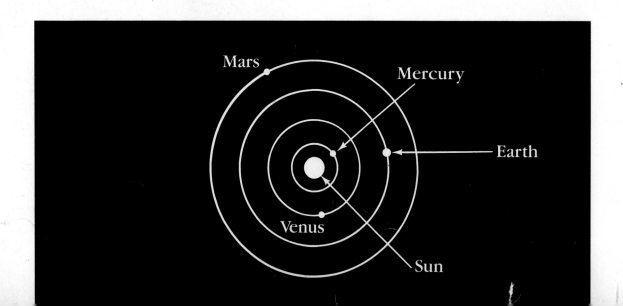

About one hundred years ago, an Italian astronomer named Giovanni Schiaparelli looked at Mars through his telescope. He thought he saw some straight, dark lines on the surface of the planet. He called them *canali*, the Italian word for channels.

People heard about the "canals" on Mars. They knew that canals are ditches dug by people to carry water from one place to another, so they decided that intelligent Martians must have built the canals. Some astronomers even drew maps of Mars showing long, straight canals crisscrossing the planet.

People began to imagine all kinds of living things on Mars. In 1898, author H. G. Wells's novel *The War of the Worlds* described tentacled, bug-eyed Martians that invade Earth to kill all the humans who live here. Later, many other monsters from Mars were featured in books, science-fiction magazines, movies, and television programs.

Until recent years, no one knew whether Martians really existed because details on Mars could not be

seen clearly through telescopes from Earth. But in the 1970s, four *Mariner* and two *Viking* spacecraft reached Mars. They found no canals on Mars, no cities, no intelligent Martians, and no life at all on the planet.

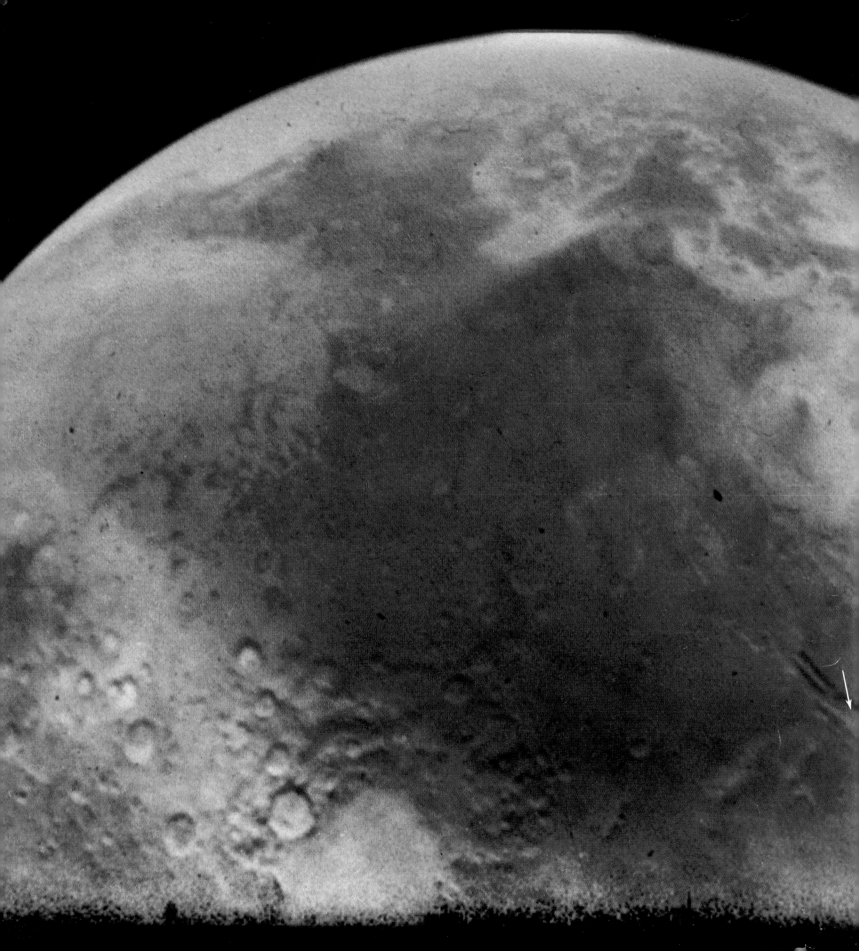

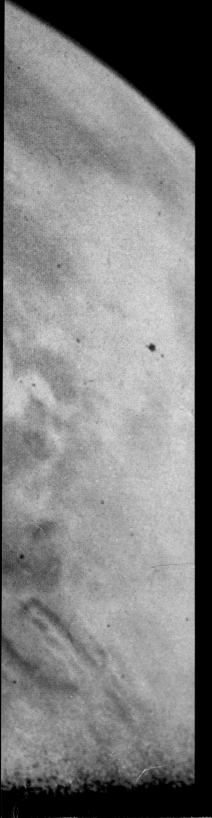

This view of Mars was sent back to Earth from one of the *Viking* spacecraft. It shows that the Martian surface has craters, mountains, volcanoes, plains, and valleys—but no straight lines. No one knows what the earlier astronomers were seeing when they thought they saw "canals." At the bottom of the photo, you can see the curving line of Mars's biggest valley, Valles Marineris. Four times as deep as the Grand Canyon of Arizona, it stretches for almost three thousand miles, about the distance from coast to coast across the United States.

Mars was once very hot inside. Molten rock, called lava, poured out on the surface, building huge volcanic peaks. This is Olympus Mons, the largest known volcano on any planet in the Solar System. It is almost three times as high as Mount Everest, the highest mountain on Earth, and its steep base would cover the entire state of Missouri. Olympus Mons is one of four giant volcanoes in a group just north of the Martian equator.

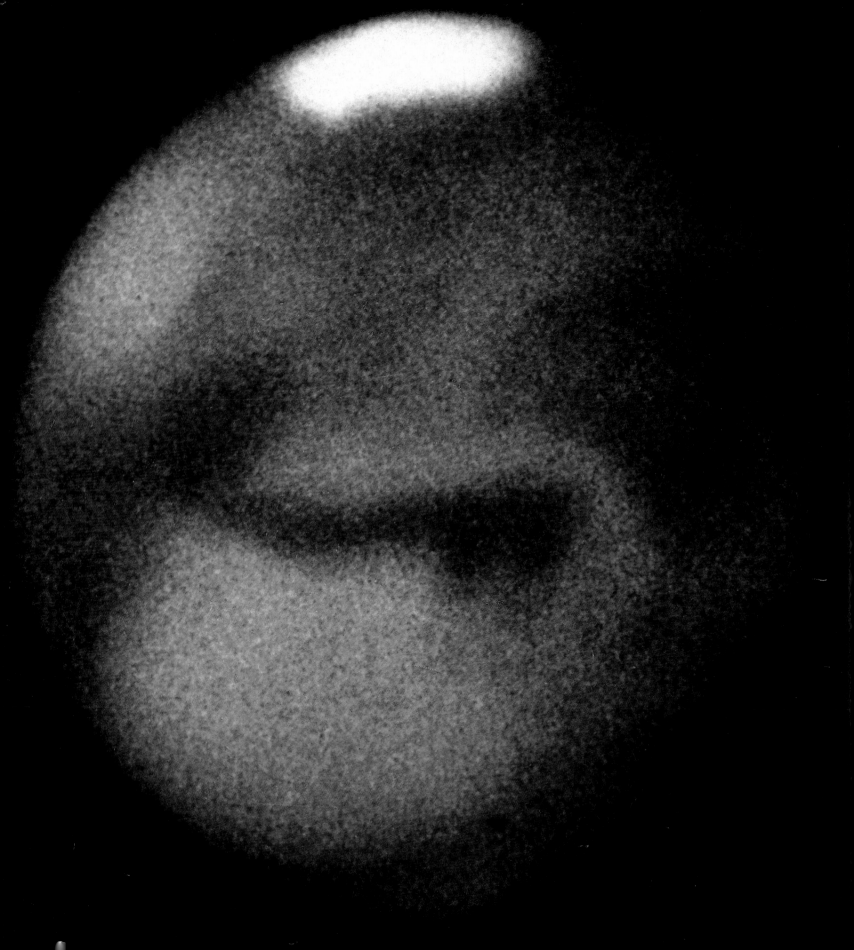

This photograph of Mars shows a polar ice cap and several large dark areas that appear greenish against the paler red surface. These dark areas grow in size during the Martian summer. Once it was thought that the green areas were covered by some kinds of plants that grew in the warmer weather. But the *Viking* space probes have shown that this is not so. There do not seem to be plants of any kind on Mars. The changes in color are the result of dust storms that hide or reveal darker materials on the surface.

Mars is a dusty planet. Its surface is covered by orange-red, dusty soil that is often moved from one spot to another by the wind. When *Mariner 9* first arrived and went into orbit around Mars, a heavy dust storm hid most of the planet. The storm raged for more than thirty days. Gradually, the dust settled down and the highest peaks poked through the haze. The black-and-white photograph shows some of the dust dunes that cover large parts of Mars. The color photograph shows places where light-colored dust conceals the darker underlying rock.

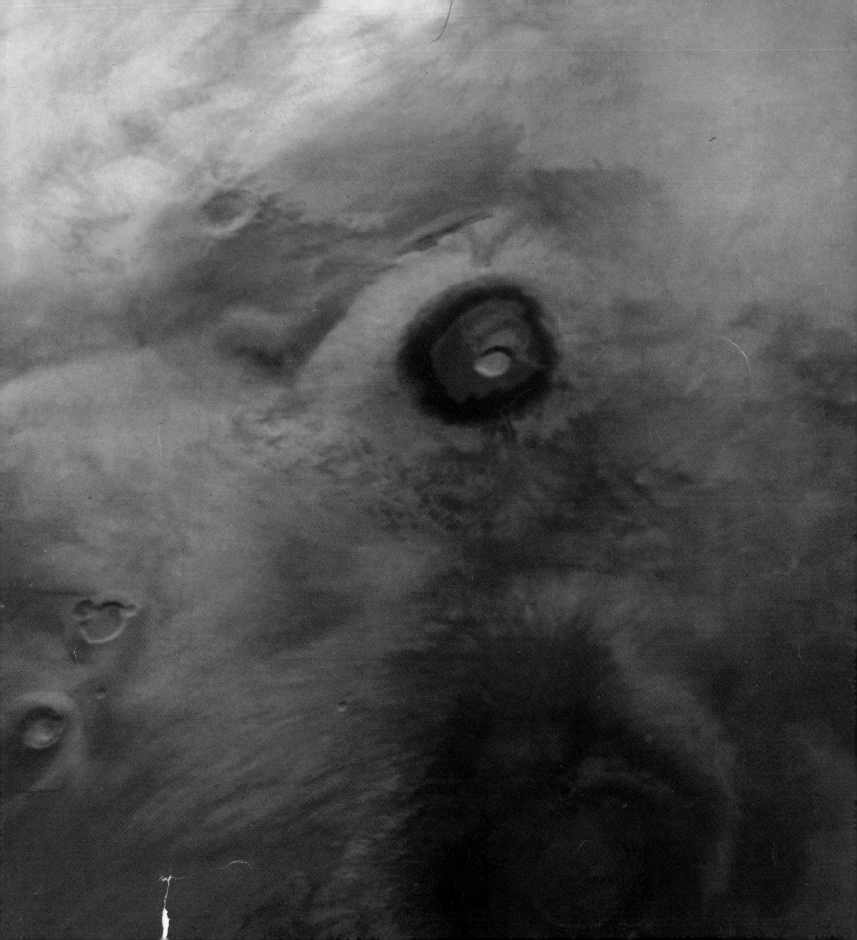

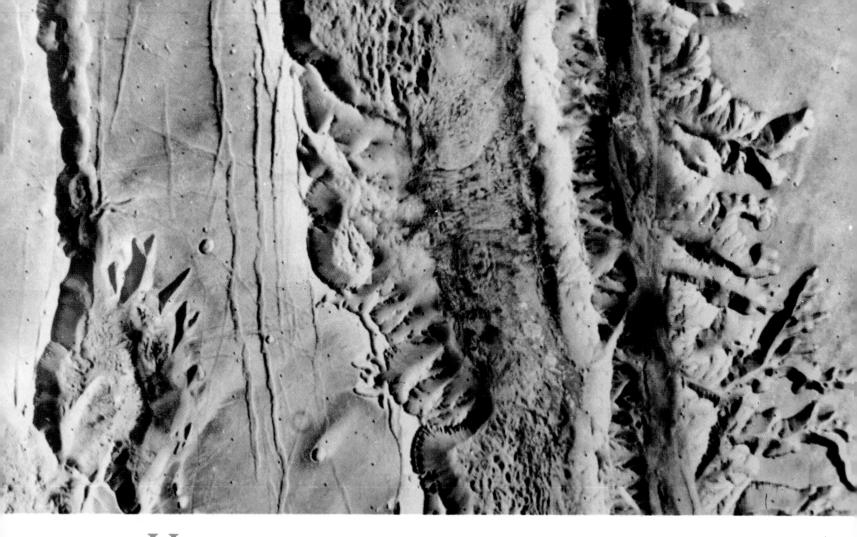

Mars may look dry as dust, but water once flowed over the surface. Millions of years ago when Mars was a young planet, it may even have had oceans. The oceans are gone, but some of the water remains hidden in large underground reservoirs. Some scientists believe that if this water came to the surface it could flood the entire planet to a depth of one thousand feet.

Many of the channels on Mars look like dry river-beds. Some of the channels cut right through meteorite craters, showing that the craters formed first. Other channels are broken by craters, showing that the craters formed later.

Even though there is no liquid water on its surface, there is lots of ice on Mars. The polar ice caps are covered by a thin layer of ice and dust. The north pole is mostly frozen water, while the south pole is ice mixed with frozen carbon dioxide, sometimes called dry ice.

This frosty scene is near Mars's north pole. Where the white ice ends and the red land begins (top part of photo) are steep cliffs about fifteen hundred feet high. The black-and-white photograph (right) shows a close-up of some of these great ice-covered cliffs.

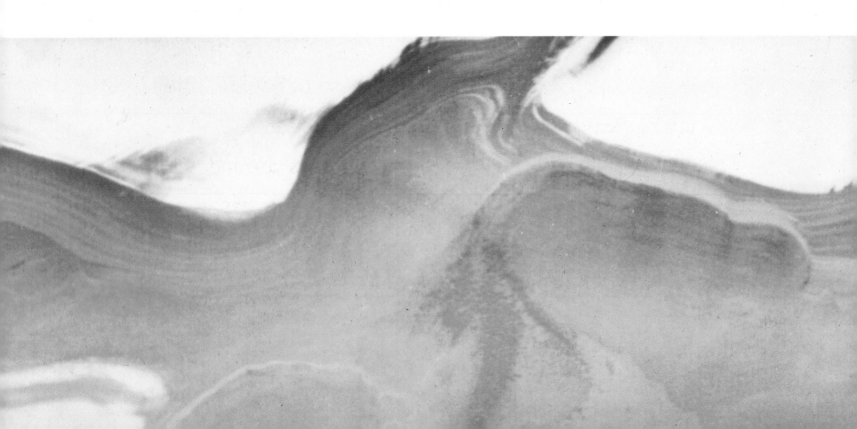

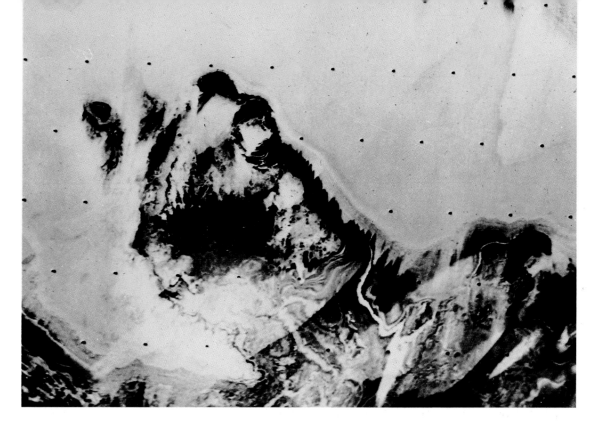

For many years, astronomers wondered why the Martian polar caps grew larger during part of the year. Now they know that the ice caps on Mars change with the seasons, like Earth's. The southern half of Mars has short, hot summers and long, cold winters. Seasons in the north are less extreme.

Mars spins on an angle as it journeys around the sun. The part that is tilted toward the sun has summer while the other part has winter. As the seasons change, the advances and retreats of the ice caps tell us about the changing climate of Mars.

Mars has two small moons, Phobos and Deimos. They are named after the two sons of Ares, the Greek god of war. Phobos [FO-bos] is the larger of the two moons and nearer to Mars. Phobos is about seventeen miles long and twelve miles wide. It races around Mars in only seven and one-half hours, at a distance of about 3,000 miles from the planet. If you were an

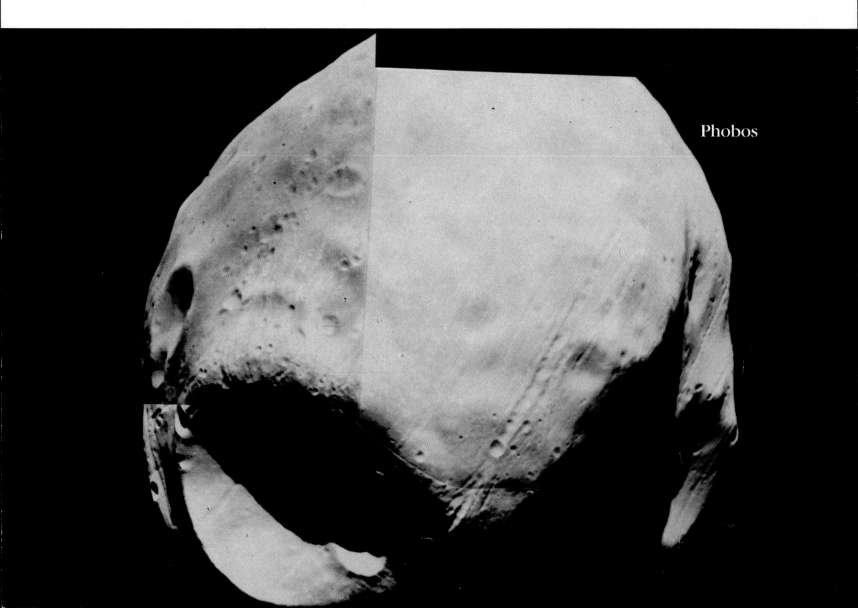

Phobos

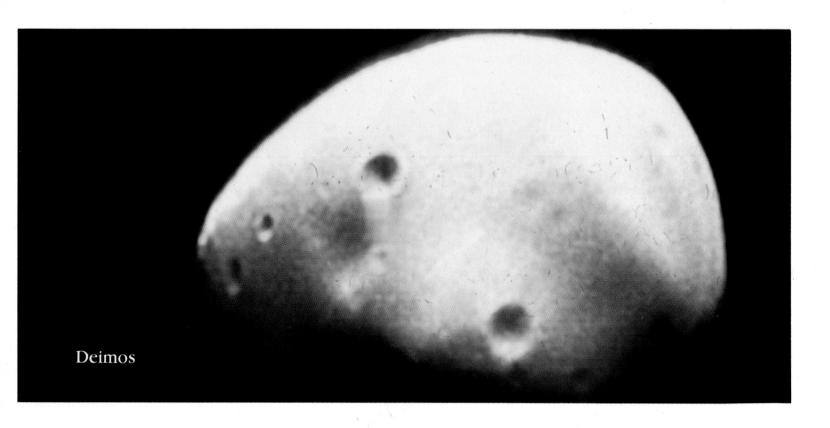

Deimos

observer on Mars, Phobos would look several times brighter than a very bright star does from Earth. The close-up photo of Phobos shows large meteorite craters and deep scratches across the surface.

Deimos [DIE-mos] is slightly smaller than Phobos, about nine miles long by seven miles wide. Deimos takes a bit longer than thirty hours to orbit Mars and is about 12,500 miles away from the planet. From the surface of Mars, Deimos would look as bright as the planet Venus does from Earth.

Viking 1 and Viking 2 were launched two weeks apart in August and September of 1975. Each Viking carried an orbiting craft and a lander. This was the United States's first attempt to land a spacecraft on another planet. The photograph shows a lander in a test site designed to look like Mars.

Traveling at tens of thousands of miles an hour, the Viking spacecraft took about ten months to reach Mars. The orbiters circled Mars for another month before the decision to land was made.

The Viking 1 lander weighed 2,633 pounds. Yet it had to come down as lightly as a feather to avoid damaging delicate instruments. The Viking 1 landing was a lucky one. Scientists had thought that the landing area was smooth and safe. But the field had many boulders nearly as large as the lander itself. If Viking 1 had set down on a boulder, it would have overturned and been damaged.

The day after it landed, *Viking 1* took this color photograph of the field on which it rested. The orange-red color is due to the chemical iron oxide, also called rust, in the dusty soil and rocks. Over the years, the *Viking* orbiters and landers sent back more than fifty thousand photos of Mars.

Even though the *Viking 2* lander came down four thousand miles away from *Viking 1*, the field of rocks looks much the same. This *Viking 2* photo was taken a few days after the lander came down on September 3, 1976.

Mars is a harsh planet for human life. The pressure of the atmosphere is so low that your blood would boil if you stepped out on the surface unprotected. You'd also have to dress very warmly. The distant sun doesn't send very much heat. The temperatures around the landers ranged from 190 degrees (F) below zero at night to 45 degrees (F) below zero in midafternoon, much colder than a deep freeze.

On the other hand, the low gravitational pull on the surface of Mars would make it easy for you to walk around in a heavy space suit. If you weigh 100 pounds on Earth, you would weigh only 38 pounds on Mars.

Is there life on Mars? The *Viking* landers were supposed to find out. Each lander had a small biology laboratory on board. Soil was scooped up by mechanical arms and brought into the lab. Three different experiments were designed to look for any traces of life in the soil. The experiments were performed several times by both landers.

Scientists are still arguing about the results of the experiments. Many scientists think the experiments show that there is no life on Mars. But other scientists believe the results are not clear. They say that while we have not discovered life on Mars, life may still exist on the planet. Perhaps Martian life is very different from life on Earth, and the landers performed the wrong kind of experiments. Or perhaps we were looking in the wrong places. Much of Mars is unexplored, and it may be quite different from the two *Viking* landing sites. Some kind of life may exist in one of these unexplored places. Just now, no one knows for sure.

This photograph of a Martian sunset was taken by the *Viking 1* lander. Someday, another probe will land on Mars and we will find out more about the mysterious red planet. And, who knows, perhaps someone reading this now will be the first human to